D0875613

Funny Laws & Other Zany Stuff

Sheryl Lindsell-Roberts

Illustrated by Myron Miller

Sterling Publishing Co., Inc.
New York

Dedicated to Max Lorenz...

My father was an ordinary man. He didn't contribute to the
world of literature, art, or science. But he was an extraordinary
father and contributed to my life immeasurably. All he had to do
was look at me or hold my hand, and I knew I was protected from
the world. I adored him.

Library of Congress Cataloging-in-Publication Data

Lindsell-Roberts, Sheryl.
    Funny laws and other zany stuff / Sheryl Lindsell-Roberts ; illustrated
by Myron Miller.
        p.   cm.
    ISBN 0-8069-2056-4
    1. Law–United States–Humor. 2. Anecdotes. I. Miller, Myron,
1948-   . II. Title
K184.L558   1999
349.73'02'97–dc21   98-56202
                                                                CIP

10 9 8 7 6 5 4 3 2 1

Published by Sterling Publishing Company, Inc.
387 Park Avenue South, New York, N.Y. 10016
© 1999 by Sheryl Lindsell-Roberts
Distributed in Canada by Sterling Publishing
⁒ Canadian Manda Group, One Atlantic Avenue, Suite 105
Toronto, Ontario, Canada M6K 3E7
Distributed in Great Britain and Europe by Cassell PLC
Wellington House, 125 Strand, London WC2R 0BB, England
Distributed in Australia by Capricorn Link (Australia) Pty Ltd.
P.O. Box 6651, Baulkham Hills, Business Centre, NSW 2153, Australia
Manufactured in the United States of America
All rights reserved

Sterling ISBN 0-8069-2056-4

Contents

From the Author

Arthur Conan Doyle, author of *The Sign of Four*, said, "When you have eliminated the impossible, whatever remains, however improbable, must be the truth." And Ethel Lorenz said, "Truth is stranger than fiction." Although my mother's words aren't original, the truth can be rather strange. Instead of questioning the origins of some truths, have fun with them.

- Why did Oklahoma pass a law making it illegal to fish for whales off its coast?
- Why does a museum in Vermont collect lint from belly buttons, dryer vents, window screens, and clothing jackets?
- Did you know that pretzels were invented by a monk to resemble children's arms folded in prayer?
- And who needs a digital watch with nearly 100 functions?

Of course, these are rhetorical questions because few, if any, have answers. However, I do hope you'll have fun with them.

Sheryl Lindsell-Roberts, M.A.

1.
TICKET TO RIDE

SORRY, SNEEZY, YOU CAN'T RIDE WITH US, WE'RE GOING THROUGH WEST VIRGINIA

HI-HO, HI-HO

Train Tribulations

In the state of West Virginia, it's against the law to sneeze on a train.

In 1895, Henry Latimer Simmons invented a railroad system that had tracks sloped on top of the cars. Trains could leapfrog over one another on a single track.

The General Services Administration spent $1.5 million—from a potential $13 million—to renovate an old, unused train station in Nashville, Tennessee. The only use the station got was as a home for a flock of roosting pigeons.

In Jamestown, North Dakota, two men sued a railroad company for $10,000. Their train was behind schedule and got them to the racetrack too late to collect the winnings from the daily double.

Alexander Sluchevsky was a wealthy resident of Kharov who traveled by rail from Ukraine to St. Petersburg once a year. He always rode on a flat car. He was seated in his own carriage, which was hitched to a team of horses. Why? He wanted to be able to continue the journey in case the train broke down.

6

There's a city ordinance in Andalusia, Alabama, prohibiting trains from running through the city at a speed faster than an ordinary citizen can walk.

This could be more than a free ride. There's a Connecticut law that the railroad must pay each passenger $25 if the passenger is delayed more than five minutes by a standing train.

New York Common Law: "A railway company which negligently throws a passenger from a crowded car onto the trestle is held liable for injury to a relative who, in going to his rescue, falls through the trestle."

Beam Me Aboard, Scotty

What will the transportation needs of earthlings be in the year 2025? Well, the Department of Transportation spent $225,000 to find out. Some questions were formulated to include transportation needs in the United States if it is

transformed by an Ice Age

taken over by a dictator

domineered by a hippie culture.

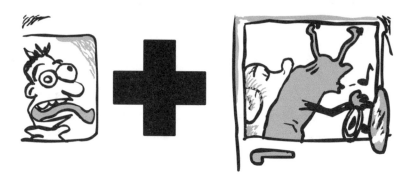

On the Road Again

In Port Huron, Michigan, the speed limit for ambulances is 20 mph.

In New Orleans, Louisiana, all fire trucks are required to stop at red lights.

In the state of Virginia pedestrians must beware! If one is struck by a moving automobile, the pedestrian—not the driver—will be fined.

Every public vehicle in San Francisco, California, must be outfitted with a spittoon. That includes taxis, police cruisers, cable cars, buses, and trolleys. If the law is violated, city officials can be prosecuted.

Driving Under the Influence

Buenos Aires, Argentina, has a major problem with drunk drivers. Therefore, the Department of Motor Vehicles has started issuing licenses only if people can pass a drunk-driving test. The test involves driving at a high speed along a crooked, very wavy-lined highway after drinking two 12-ounce bottles of beer.

Keep on Trucking

Do oversized trucks block your vision on the highway? Go uphill slowly? Contribute to traffic congestion? Make a big splash on wet roads? The Federal Highway Administration spent $222,000 to find out the astonishing answers. You bet they do! We could have told them that for a fraction the price.

Up, Up and Away

There's a law in Maine that prohibits anyone from stepping out of a plane while it's in the air.

It's illegal for an airplane to fly over a stadium during a game in Baltimore, Maryland.

Anti-object artist, Le Ann Wilchusky, received a $6,025 grant from the National Endowment for the Arts for this: She boarded a small aircraft, armed with a large bundle of crepe-paper streamers. The plane took off, and at the appropriate moment, Ms. Wilchusky threw the streamers out into the sky. She later told reporters: "I'm sculpting in space. A black streamer looks like a crack in the sky. Red and yellow streamers look like high lines, lashing the earth. By making people look upward, my work called attention to the higher spirit of mankind."

2.
TELL IT TO THE JUDGE

Order in the Court

An Iowa woman was accused of stealing a $25 sweater. Shortly thereafter, agents confiscated her $18,000 car that was specially equipped to transport her handicapped daughter. They claimed the vehicle was used as the getaway car.

A judge in Worcester, Massachusetts, responded to the plea of a thief claiming he stole while under hypnosis. The judge advised the defendant to get re-hypnotized so he wouldn't mind spending 10 years in jail.

Bert Winkler, of Yazoo City, Mississippi, was brought to trial on charges of bank robbery. He convinced a friend to slip the jurors a note saying he'd give them each $1,000 if they acquitted him. After he was found not guilty, Winkler gave each juror $1,000, the judge $5,000, and the bailiff $250. He even gave $5 to each person who attended the trial, and gave the prosecuting attorney a nickel.

The Law Enforcement Assistance Administration spent $27,000 on a study to determine why inmates escape from jail. The real crime was wasting $27,000 for the study.

Athens, Georgia: A new prison warden was assigned to the state penitentiary. He gathered all the inmates and told them: "Although you are criminals, I believe you're still entitled to some rights." Unfortunately, his Southern drawl made it difficult for him to be understood and the prisoners thought he said, "You're still entitled to some riots." For the next six hours the prisoners tore the prison apart.

During a Fourth of July weekend, a woman drove to her Boston neighborhood and spent two and a half hours looking for a parking space. She desperately needed to use the bathroom, so she double parked in front of her apartment and ran in quickly. When she returned, she found that her car had been towed away.

A woman in Norfolk, Nebraska, was brought to court for crossing the street against a red light. For this infraction she was fined $2.50. The woman gave the clerk a $5 bill and turned around to leave before receiving her change. When the judge called after her, she turned around and said: "That's okay, I need to cross back to the other side."

A woman in Haleiwa, Hawaii, was stopped on Highway 83 by a police officer for going 65 mph in a 45 mph zone. She appealed the case and told the judge she was rushing home because she had to take her birth control pill "before it's too late." The judge admitted the originality of her allegation, but fined her anyway.

In the Eyes of the Beholder

If you want to use curlers in your hair in Oklahoma, you'd better have a curl license.

In Michigan, a woman's hair belongs to her husband.

There's an ordinance in Morrisville, Pennsylvania, that prohibits a woman from wearing cosmetics without a permit.

Inane Insurance Claims

These were taken from reports that policyholders were asked to fill out following automobile accidents:

The pedestrian had no idea which direction to go, so I ran over him.

Coming home, I drove into the wrong house and collided with a tree I didn't have.

The accident happened when the right front door of a car came around the corner without giving a signal.

The telephone pole was approaching fast. I was attempting to swerve out of its path when it struck my front end.

I was on the way to the doctor's with rear-end trouble when my universal joint gave way causing me to have an accident.

The guy was all over the road. I had to swerve a couple of times before I hit him.

The Envelope, Please

California has finally answered the long-awaited question "What's the State Dirt?" As of January 1, 1998, the Official State Dirt is San Joaquin (san-wä-'ken) soil.

3.
IN THE NAME OF LOVE

Together Again

Mr. and Mrs. Chip Stalter were married on March 11, 1985, in Hillsdale, New Jersey. So what, you might ask? Well, they were both born on October 21, 1959, in the same hospital, and their moms shared a room. Their mothers hadn't kept in touch.

Endless Engagement

In Russia, Svetlana Korchnoi and Ivan Rostropovich have been engaged for more than 41 years. They met in a borscht factory, fell in love, and still work there. They claim they'll get married as soon as they can afford to move out of their parents' homes.

Legal Brief

Two attorneys in Hartford, Connecticut, wrote their own wedding vows. The vows of Bernard Prothroe and Annamarie Kendall covered 47 single-spaced, 8½ x 14-inch typewritten pages. It took the officiator more than five hours to read them. By the time the ceremony was over, 90 percent of the guests had left, including the parents of the bride and groom.

Amour

In Logan County, Colorado, a man isn't allowed to kiss a woman while she's asleep.

If you plan to walk down the street with another man's wife, you'd better stay away from Challis, Idaho. It's illegal.

In Eureka, Nevada, men who have mustaches are forbidden to kiss women.

"Why Do Fools Fall in Love?" The National Science Institute wanted to find out why and for how long males and females are attracted to each other and spent $84,000 on this study. (*Can anyone tell us the results?*)

In Little Rock, Arkansas, members of the opposite sex can be thrown in jail for 30 days for flirting.

There's a romantic drive-in theater in New Mexico that only shows romantic movies, attaches a red rose to the speaker of each car, sells champagne and chocolate at the snack bar, and has a violinist strolling by the cars playing special requests.

In Truro, Mississippi, before a man gets married he must "prove himself worthy" by hunting and killing either six blackbirds or three crows.

And Baby Makes Three

It's against the law for children under the age of seven to go to college in Winston-Salem, North Carolina.

Although there are no *R* and *X* ratings for Ma Bell, in Blue Earth, Minnesota, it's against the law for children under 12 to talk on the telephone unless accompanied by a parent.

In Kampuchea, a hamlet of Paoy Pet, children outnumber adults five to one. The voting age is seven, and the mayor is only nine. Because children rule, they can punish their parents if they've been bad.

Kids in Kalispell, Montana, must have a note from the doctor in order to buy a lollipop or candy bar while church services are in session.

At the Paiute Indian Reservation in California, a mother-in-law is prohibited from spending more than 30 days a year visiting her kids.

The six-year-old son of the mayor in Tadmor, Syria, was kidnapped by terrorists. The mayor refused to pay ransom, claiming that his son was always misbehaving. The boy behaved so badly, the terrorists returned him for the equivalent of 50¢ and the mayor's promise not to prosecute.

4.
<u>LAW AND ORDER</u>

These lawsuits are a matter of public record. They're intended to entertain, not embarrass, so some names have been changed and (in some cases) venues omitted.

Ghost Buster

Case: Sylvester bought his $650,000 dream house in a small village. When the architect refused to work on changes, Sylvester learned that the the seller had written an article in the local newspaper and *Reader's Digest* saying that the house was inhabited by a ghost who ate ham sandwiches. Sylvester took this case to the Appeals Court demanding the return of his $32,500 deposit.

Ruling: The judge ruled against Sylvester. Why? The fact that the former owner had aired the story publicly meant that "as a matter of law, the house is haunted." *Caveat emptor* (buyer beware) reigned supreme. So, when you're buying a house, perhaps you should call Ghost Busters. (Think they'd be in the Yellow Pages?)

Stick 'Em Up

Case: An unemployed poet in Port Said, Egypt, was in love with a bank teller and sent her love letters for several years. Mustafa Hazez received no replies from the teller, and decided to be more aggressive. He went to the bank and approached the teller with a gun and love letter, demanding that she declare her love for him or hand over all the money in her drawer. She gave him the money and he was brought up on charges.

Ruling: Hazez was, of course, convicted of robbery and sentenced to jail. He was given a suspended sentence, however, on the grounds of temporary insanity.

19

HEY GRACE, (TEE HEE) I HEAR YOU TOOK ONE "WRITE" IN THE STOMACH.

This Is No Gag

Case: Grace worked as a receptionist in a doctor's office where doughnuts were routinely brought in for the staff. One morning a doughnut made her ill. Grace induced vomiting, putting a pen down her throat, and accidentally swallowed the pen. She was rushed to the hospital and operated on, but was unable to work for three weeks. Grace filed for workers' compensation.

Ruling: Workers' compensation was granted by a district court judge. The Appeals Court reversed the decision, stating that: "Putting a pen down one's throat to induct vomiting is a risk. It isn't an occupational hazard of a receptionist in a doctor's office."

Iced

Case: Parviz Mahin, a janitor at a bus depot in Ankara, Turkey, found a bag of precious stones worth $7.3 million. A Good Samaritan, he returned the stones to the jeweler. The jeweler didn't offer any reward. Mr. Mahin asked the jeweler for a small diamond ring for his wife. The jeweler refused, and Mr. Mahin took a ring. The jeweler pressed charges.

Ruling: Mr. Mahin had to spend six years in jail.

Where There's a Will...

Case: In Mahdia, Tunisia, a 67-year-old philanthropist died, leaving his worldly goods to his wife, nine children, 13 grandchildren, aunts, uncles, nieces, nephews, friends, business associates, mailman, secretary, etc. He didn't, however, include his gardener or his barber. They've contested the will.

Ruling: The case is pending, and so far no one's collected a cent.

Shoplifting at Bargain Prices

Case: A 32-year-old woman in Rutland County, Vermont, was picked up for shoplifting in a supermarket. She had helped herself to $101.49 worth of batteries, cigarettes, doughnuts, and videotapes. The woman was charged with a felony, punishable by up to 10 years in jail. Her public defender filed a motion asking the court to reduce the theft to a misdemeanor, which was punishable by a maximum of six months in jail. Apparently the threshold for a felony charge is $100 and the public defender claimed that the batteries and doughnuts were on sale, so the theft totaled only $97.37, just under the $100 threshold.

Ruling: The judge "bought it." The woman's charges were reduced to a misdemeanor.

5.
GROUNDS
FOR DIVORCE

"Marriage may be compared to a cage: the birds outside despair to get in and those within despair to get out."
—Michel de Montaigne, *Essays*

Although divorce is never funny, some of the allegations are—regardless of the outcome. Here are some loony allegations from "her side" and "his."

SO..., YOU CAN **KISS** YOUR MONEY GOODBYE.

Her Side

Marshfield, Wisconsin: When the couple married, he promised to pay her $1 for each kiss as long as they remained married. She sued him for divorce and asked the court for an award of $3,000 in back payments.

Susanville, California: She sued him for divorce because he sold the kitchen stove in order to get the money to purchase liquor to feed his habit. He owned up to the fact that he did sell the stove, but begged the court for leniency because she didn't miss the stove for two weeks.

Pendleton, Oregon: She sued him for divorce because he never gave her Christmas presents. He claimed to be confident that Santa would bring them.

Winnemucca, Nevada: She snatched a letter from the postman that was in her husband's handwriting. When she opened the letter, she realized it was a love letter to another woman. She sued for divorce and won but had to pay a fine of $20 for tampering with the mail.

Strawberry Plains, Tennessee: She petitioned the court for divorce because she served steak and onions for dinner regularly. The problem was that he ate the steak and left her the onions.

Canon City, Colorado: She sued him on the grounds that he forced her to hide under the dashboard of his automobile whenever he passed a girlfriend.

23

His Side

Price, Utah: He petitioned the court for a divorce because she insisted on hanging the pictures of her four ex-husbands over the bed.

Point Charlotte, Florida: He filed for divorce immediately after they'd taken their vows. Why? Immediately after their *I do's,* she took him to her favorite bar and said to the bartender: "I told you I'd marry him. Now give me the $50."

Montevideo, Minnesota: He sued her for divorce on the grounds that she didn't love him. It seems he fell down the basement steps and was sprawled on the floor in a semi-conscious state. She rushed to the scene and said, "While you're down there, put some coal in the furnace."

Huntingburg, Indiana: They met through a lonely-hearts advertisement and married before they had actually seen each other. She claimed to be five feet tall and 118 pounds, but she was actually six feet tall and weighed 300 pounds. He sued for divorce on the grounds of false advertising.

Platteville, Wisconsin: He filed for divorce after her plane trip. It seems she took out travel insurance and named their dog as beneficiary.

Grants, New Mexico: He sued her for divorce because of her extramarital affairs. The court blamed the husband, claiming that he knew of her yen for other men and should have "exercised a peculiar vigilance over her."

Rock Springs, Wyoming: Right after they had tied the knot, she admitted that she had married him for his money. He angrily filed for divorce. However, his divorce was denied because the judge explained, "The game laws of the state provide no closed season against this kind of trapping."

Forever Hold Your Peace

Representative Linda Larason, from Oklahoma, was concerned about the divorce rate being so high. So she proposed a law stating that before a couple be issued a marriage license, they sign a contract agreeing to the following:

Neither shall snore.

At least one meal a week shall be prepared by the non-primary cook.

Toothpaste will be squeezed from the bottom of the tube and the cap shall always be put back on.

Pantyhose can't be left hanging in the shower.

And the toilet seat shall always be down when not being used.

Mr. Clean

Case: Barbara sued Timothy for divorce on the grounds that he did all the housework and cooking. Barbara wasn't allowed to shop, clean house, or slave over a hot stove in the 13 years they were married. She hated living on a pedestal and charged Timothy with cruelty.

Ruling: She lost! The judge ruled that Timothy "has been tactless, not cruel."

Blab, Blab, Blab

Case: Lee and Roberta had been married for 40 years when he took up with another woman. A divorce suit followed. Lee argued that it was all Roberta's fault because she had nagged him during their entire marriage and her "harassment, accusations, and nagging" caused him to fly into the arms of another.

Ruling: The Appeals Court ruled that after 40 years, he was carrying this a little too far. However, Roberta did not get alimony; that was the price she had to pay for the tongue lashings.

Big Bride and Grim Groom

Case: Fred and Olga were married only a month when Fred filed for divorce. He claimed the marriage should never have taken place. He was drunk at the wedding, having tippled two gallons of beer. During an argument, his 250-pound wife knocked him to the floor and sat on him for 10 minutes. He sued for divorce on the grounds of "cruel and inhuman treatment." Olga claimed that Fred wasn't pushed, rather that he fell and she sat in his lap.

Ruling: The judge granted Fred the divorce.

6.
JUST FER FUN

Chuck It

The World Cow Chip Throwing Contest is held in Oklahoma each year. You'll see grown men competing to see which one can toss a lump of cow droppings the farthest.

Fiddling Around

Each year Florida sponsors the International Worm Fiddling Contest. Contestants drive a stake into the ground and rub it with an object that makes it vibrate. This makes worms come to the surface.

My Gal Sal

A visit to Salley, South Carolina, wouldn't be complete without attending the Chitlin Strut. Chitlins—hog intestines that are boiled or fried—are consumed by the ton at this festival.

Flipping Out

If you want to run 415 yards down a Main Street flipping pancakes, you might visit Liberal, Kansas, when the town features the all-women's International Pancake Race.

WAIT, CAN WE HAVE THAT FOR OUR MUSEUM?

While You're in the Neighborhood

In Rutland, Vermont, visit the International Lint Museum, which displays lint from belly buttons, dryer vents, window screens, and clothing pockets.

If you don't want to visit the Ben & Jerry's Ice Cream Factory in Vermont, participate in the World Shovel Championship Race. You can spend half an hour riding a coal-type shovel downhill at 40 to 50 miles per hour. Or skip over New Hampshire and roll over to Maine to participate in the World Heavyweight Championship Ski Race. There are restrictions, however. You must weigh a minimum of 225, though typical contestants weigh in at 450+ pounds.

Don't Miss Issippi

You can attend the National Tobacco Spit, where contests are held for spitting accuracy and distance. Or you might consider the Leake County Sportsmen's Day where ladies climb greasy poles and compete for the much-sought-after title of Miss Freckles.

Really a Prince

The next time you're in Arkansas, visit the Frog Fantasies Museum where 5,000 frogs are on display. The museum sponsors a contest, so you have a chance to write about your own personal "Frog Fantasies." (*Perhaps one of the 5,000 frogs is really a handsome prince.*)

Scream and Shout

You might want to hone your vocal chords before you participate in the National Hollerin' Contest in North Carolina. Men vie for the honor of being able to scream the loudest and women go lung-to-lung in a calling event.

Ain't This Duck-y

The Cask County Quack-Off is held each year in Nebraska where you can race ducks on the ice. If you don't own one, you can rent a canard for the day. If that doesn't suit you, you might try The Muzzle-Loaders Rendezvous or The Middle of Nowhere Parade.

If You'd Rather Go Abroad...

Each year, Coxheath, England, holds its pie throwing contest. Competitors are required to throw a pie 9 feet, hitting the (human) face of the target.

Run the Numbers

In Viola, Minnesota, there's an appalling contest called the Gopher Count. It's shared by thousands of participants who rally in the town of Viola with the gophers they've killed. The person turning in the largest number of gopher's feet wins a cash prize. Or you can attend the Grumpy Old Men Festival and hope Ann Margret shows up.

Take Your Pick

If you're passing through Iowa, you have a number of fun options. There's the annual B-Brrry Scurry-b-Brrry Fest, the Porktoberfest, Ackley Sauerkraut Days, or the Hobo Convention.

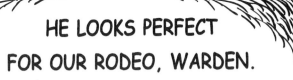

Don't Con Me

Texas hosts the "Dang'est Show on Earth," a Prison Rodeo. More than 100,000 spectators gather each year to watch convicts attempt some of the most dangerous rodeo events.

Texas also hosts the Luling Watermelon Thump, where participants join a car rally. They follow directions and master watermelon-stealing techniques.

Playing Possom

Here's your chance to display your pet possum before a panel of experts. Stop by in Alabama for that chance.

7.
MOTHER'S THE NECESSITY OF INVENTION

In 1899, Charles H. Duell, Commissioner of the United States Patent Office, wanted to close the Patent Office. He said, "Everything that can be invented has been invented."

However...

"No More Cake for You!"

There's a scale that has a memory and can be programmed with a vocabulary of up to 230 words. When you weigh yourself, it'll remember what you weighed last and either praise or scold you until you reach your target weight. (I didn't bother to find out where to get one, so don't ask.)

Chicken Specks

Chickens are known to be nasty birds and injure each other severely when they're cooped up. So Andrew Jackson, Jr. invented eye protectors for chickens that are worn like eyeglasses. And they are adjustable to fit chickens of any size or type.

Flip Your Lid

Would you like to wear a hat with a lid that could be raised or lowered by a wire in your pocket? Johann Smith-Blank invented such a top hat to keep himself cool on sizzling hot days.

HEY, DUCKY,
COOL
SHOTGUN.

Just Duck-y

Can a hunter make a killing wearing a stuffed bird resembling whatever animal he's hunting? Raymond E. Norris thought so. He was granted a patent for a cape that hangs around the hunter from the sides of a cap. The hunter's head and body movements increase the lifelike nature of the decoy, and critters are expected to come flocking.

Fire Escape

A gent by the name of Oppenheimer invented a hat parachute and padded shoes so a person would be able to jump safely from a tall building if it was on fire. The inventor forgot to consider that the wind could carry the jumper toward the burning building or that the chin buckle could choke the wearer.

Don't Oversleep

In 1907, the U.S. Patent Office granted a patent to a man who invented an alarm clock that sprayed water on the face of the sleeping person.

And then there's Samuel Applegate, who wanted to be certain everyone could wake up on time. So he attached 60 corks to a piece of string and hung the contraption above the head of a sleeping person. This contraption was connected to a clock. When the clock signaled that it was time for the sleeper to wake up, the cork contraption would fall on the sleeper's head. The blow was enough to awaken the sleeper, but not cause injury.

Double or Nothing

In 1953, Howard Ross, of Gainesville, Virginia, patented a topcoat that could be worn by one person or could double as a coat for two.

A Hairy One

Edwin O'Brien invented a set of three mirrors so people can see the back of their head. You slip on a jacket and plug in the mirrors for illumination. This is intended to provide a 360-degree view so you can brush your hair and see what you look like from three angles.

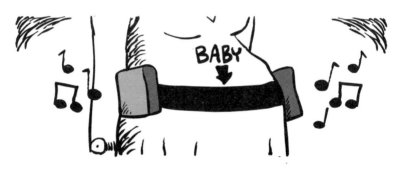

Baby's First Words

Douglas C. Fox invented a fetal speaker system that fastens around the abdomen of the mom-to-be. It's somewhat like a support belt with a pair of low-volume speakers mounted on it. A radio is maintained in position by a sturdy sleeve on the side of the belt. (I wonder what the baby's first words would be if the mom listens to Howard Stern regularly?

Crazy Carriage

George Clark designed an unusual baby carriage. It looks like a high-button shoe with wheels underneath and an umbrella on top. Mr. Clark hoped that wealthy people would enjoy pushing their children around town in something that others didn't have.

So Much for the Stork

George and Charlotte Blonsky invented a centrifugal delivery table. First, the mother-to-be is strapped to the table. Then the table spins and spins, using centrifugal force to encourage the baby to emerge. Wonder how many kids they have?

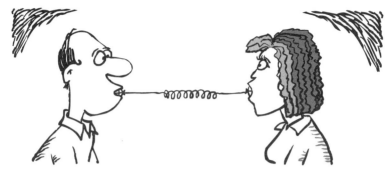

Mouth to Mouth

The merits of exercise have long been lauded, but Charles G. Purdy took this to another level. How about a devise to maintain the necessary circulation of the mouth? Here's how it works: A plate is gripped between the teeth of two people and a flexible spring connects the plates. Each person pulls in the opposite direction for an oral tug of war.

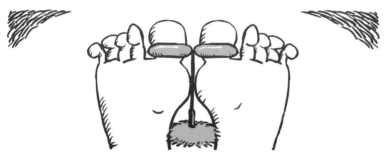

Tropical Tan

Russell Greathouse was concerned that people weren't getting "even" tans at the beach because their feet were spread apart. So he invented connected toe rings that sunbathers would place on their big toes to keep their feet together.

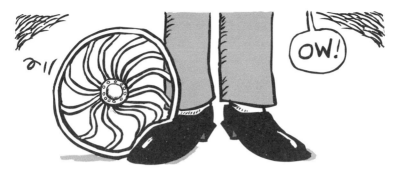

Reinventing the Wheel

Sydney Jones of Great Malvern, England, did just that. He invented a wheel that was made of elastic spring steel. Its rim folds around obstacles and rolls over them, somewhat like an air cushion.

Conspicuous Consumption, Ltd.

Yes, that's the name of a company in Beverly Hills. The company rents a unique Cadillac limousine that seats 12; has a full bar, refrigerator, microwave oven; a satellite dish on the roof, large television screen, VCR; pinball machine, library, PC, and telescope. The roof slides back to accommodate a hideaway hot tub. All this for just $1,000 an hour.

Time Flies, Smokes, and Analyzes

Tempus Fugit, Inc. of Sheffield, England, invented a digital watch with nearly 100 functions. In addition to telling the date and time, this timepiece has a smoke detector, bottle opener, and air-quality analyzer. It can also take your blood pressure, alcohol and blood level, and pulse rate.

No More Dirty Birds

Bertha Dlugi was a "neat freak." She wanted to make sure her bird's cage stayed spotless so she invented bird diapers that could be secured with a tiny clasp. The bird's legs and wings were free so it didn't restrict the bird in any way. The diapers were available in various sizes to fit any type of bird.

Great Gills

The U.S. Office of Naval Research is working on the "hemosponge." It's an experimental devise that may make it possible for divers to remain submerged for several days, extracting oxygen from the water.

Noble Nobel

Did you know that the Nobel Peace Price was named after Alfred B. Nobel? The irony of is that Mr. Nobel was the inventor of dynamite, which caused the death of millions of soldiers in wars all over the world.

The Walls Have Eyes

There was an invention many years ago that permitted people to see through walls. Have any idea what it is?

A window

I LIKE THE "MUFF" PART ...BUT,...

Did You Know...?

Ear muffs were invented by Chester Greenwood, a young man of 15.

Samuel F. B. Morse invented the telegraph and Morse code because news of his wife's death arrived by mail, seven days late.

There's a contraption for making dimples. It was patented in 1896 by M. Goetze.

Pretzels were invented by monks in Southern France in 610 A.D. to look like children's arms folded in prayer.

The word "sandwich" was coined after the Earl of Sandwich. He was playing a card game and wanted a meal that wouldn't interrupt his game.

Thomas Edison invented a sewing machine that was voice powered. He felt that women would "rather talk than treadle."

The toothbrush was invented by an inmate in the 1770s. William Addis bore holes in a small bone, tied stiff bristles into tufts, and inserted the bristles in the holes.

Hollywood makeup artist Max Factor first became known when he invented a kissing machine in the 1930s. It had rubber molded lips that were pressed together to test lipstick.

The hourglass was invented for the sole purpose of limiting the length of sermons.

Street Quibble

What is the most common street?

a) Elm Street

b) Main Street

c) Canal Street

d) None of the above

If you guessed d), you'd be correct. The most common street shares the name of the person who invented the modern process of paving. It's John McAdam of Scotland, and the street is macadam.

Who's the Inventor?

Who discovered or invented the rocking chair, daylight savings time, the street lamp, electricity, the harmonica, the glass harmonica, marsh gas, the circulating library, the benefits of fresh air, the corn broom, the aurora borealis, vitamins in the sun's rays, white duck clothing, and (here's the giveaway) the Franklin stove?

Benjamin Franklin

8.
WHAT'S UP, DOC?

A young woman named Caroline Carnes was admitted to the Seychelles Hospital for an appendectomy. The staff confused her with someone else, and sent her to the mental ward. She spent three days in a straightjacket before she was able to convince the attendants that they'd made a mistake. She was finally brought to the operating room and her chart got lost. The doctor removed her large intestine. She didn't realize the mistake until a few months later when her appendix started bothering her again.

A Cambodian man named Dith Pang has a tongue that measures 11¾ inches long when it's fully extended. He's learned to talk with his teeth clenched so his tongue won't roll out. And his mother claims that when he was a young boy, he'd imitate frogs by catching flies with his tongue.

The Food and Drug Administration (FDA) has refused to approve a pump that can save the lives of heart attack victims. This device has been so successful in Austria and France that it's mandatory ambulance equipment in these countries. Why is the FDA refusing? The agency insists that the pumpmakers get the "informed consent" of any patient on whom the pump is tested. That's not likely to happen because at the point this pump would be effective, the victims are clinically dead.

Horace MacIntyre attended Albert Einstein High School in Seattle, Washington. He was an avid scientist and won many awards for his inventions. For his final science project, Horace built an antigravity molecular phase shifter and used it to levitate his science teacher, Mabel Simpson. He received only a *B* on his project because Ms. Simpson came down so hard she broke her ankle.

A man in Eau Claire, Wisconsin, had promised a local medical group that he would one day donate his body for research. When the man had two teeth pulled, the medical group sued him because he did so without their permission.

Cece Leclere has what scientists call "megavision." This Basel, Switzerland, woman can see through manila envelopes, clothing, and brick walls. She claims that people often make her sick because she can look at their internal organs and it nauseates her.

Does Your Mummy Know You're Out?

University of Virginia: Dr. Raymond Tolbert, an archaeology professor, was deeply depressed when his mother died. So he embalmed her, wrapped her up, and takes mummy wherever he goes. Since then, his depression has been cured.

Dead or Alive?

A sailor from Annapolis, Maryland, was missing for a long time and was declared legally dead. When he turned up alive many years later, he found that all his assets had been divided among his relatives. Despite a 10-year bout in the courts, he never came back to life legally—except that his existence was acknowledged by the Internal Revenue Service.

9.
AS I WAS SAYING...

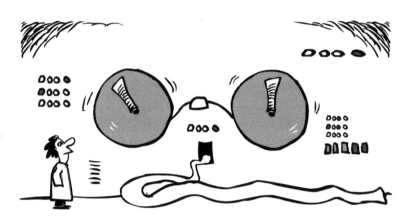

Man and Machine

"Computers in the future may weigh no more than 1.5 tons."   —*Popular Mechanics*, 1949

"I think there is a world market for maybe five computers."   —Thomas Watson, Chairman of IBM, 1943

"But what is it [the microchip] good for?"
  —Engineer, Advanced Computing Systems, IBM, 1968

"This telephone has too many shortcomings to be seriously considered as a means of communication. This device is inherently of no value to us."
              —Western Union internal memo, 1876

"The wireless music box has no imaginable commercial value. Who would pay for a message sent to nobody in particular?"
              —David Sarnoff's associates, in response to
                his urgings to invest in the radio, 1920

"The concept [reliable overnight delivery service] is interesting and well formed, but in order to earn better than a *C*, the idea must be feasible."
  —Yale professor, in response to Fred Smith's paper.
    (Smith went on to found Federal Express.)

"So we went to Atari and said, 'Hey, we've got this amazing thing, even built with some of your parts, and what do you think about funding us? Or we'll give it to you. We just want to do it. Pay our salary, we'll come to work for you.' And they said, 'No.' So we went to Hewlett-Packard, and they said, 'We don't need you. You haven't gone to college yet.'"
— Steve Jobs (founder of Apple Computer, Inc.)

"640K ought to be enough for anybody."
— Bill Gates (founder of Microsoft, Inc.), 1981

That's Entertainment

"Who the hell wants to hear actors talk?"
— H. M. Warner, Warner Brothers, 1927

"I'm glad it'll be Clark Gable who's falling on his face and not me."
— Gary Cooper (when he declined the leading role in *Gone With The Wind*)

"We don't like their sound, and guitar music is on the way out."
— Decca Recording Co. (rejecting the Beatles), 1962

10.
OLD MACDONALD'S <u>BARNYARD</u>

Horsin' Around

In Waco, Texas, it's illegal to toss a banana peel on the streets because a horse could step on the peel and slip.

The U.S. Air Force bestowed upon the University of Florida a $100,000 grant to see if the noise of low-flying F-4 Phantom fighter jets would have a negative effect on pregnant horses in the Southwest.

If you're in the market for a horse, you might want to visit Virginia when it sponsors the Assateague Pony Swim. A herd of ponies is forced to swim to Assateague Island. Then they're driven down main street and auctioned off.

If you're a motorist passing through Pennsylvania and sight a team of horses coming toward you, you must pull well off the road, cover your car with a blanket or canvas that blends in with the countryside, and let the horses pass. If one of the horses is skittish, you must take your car apart piece by piece and hide it under the nearest bush.

If you're riding through Charleston, South Carolina, your horse better be wearing diapers.

In Maysville, West Virginia, horses command the greatest respect. There's a law mandating that anyone meeting a horse and buggy on the road must bow from the waist.

In 1876, I.M.S.R. Mathewson, of Gilroy California, invented a gasoline motor that looked like a horse. His explanation was: "So it would not frighten real horses."

M-I-C...K-E-Y M o u s e

In Comal County, Texas, Mickey Mouse is prohibited from running for public office. This is why. "Mickey Mouse is not and has not been a resident of Comal County for six months as required by law...and is, there-fore, under the laws of Texas, ineligible to hold office."

The Bear Facts

The Department of the Interior was responsible for passing the Endangered Species Act. As a result, a Montana rancher named John Shuler was stiffly fined for shooting a bear that attacked him on his own land.

Here's the scoop: Grizzly bears had been mauling Mr. Shuler's sheep for months. One night he heard a dis-turbance; he grabbed his gun and ran outside. He saw four grizzlies. Three were attacking his sheep and one was running toward him. Mr. Shuler shot the bear and ran back to his home for safety. The judge fined him $4,000, declaring him at fault because "he purposefully placed himself in the zone of imminent danger."

An employee at the U.S. Forest Service receives an annual salary in excess of $42,000 to oversee the trade-mark the government holds on Smokey the Bear.

Holy Cow!

Men in Fruithill, Kentucky, must remove their hats when they come face to face with a cow.

This is no bull! There's a law in Leadville, Colorado, that describes how a bull must be equipped while walking on a highway. He must wear a bell, whistle or horn, headlight, and tail light.

In the 19th century, Juanito Apinani, a matador from Spain, thrilled the crowds and won a bullfight by using his lance to leap over the charging bull.

Livin' High on the Hog

How should a pregnant pig be treated? And would she be less bored if she jogged? The U.S. Department of Agriculture (USDA) studied sows that were cooped up during pregnancy, and they noticed that all kinds of problems surfaced. The pigs suffered from tension and a lack of exercise. So, the USDA devised treadmills for them, to reduce the psychological stress on these mommies-to-be.

Playing Chicken

Gainesville, Georgia, considers itself the "Chicken Capital of the World," and it's illegal there to eat chicken with a fork.

In Kankakee, Illinois, a woman brought charges against a masher because he called her a *chicken*. The judge asked the woman how much she weighed, calculated what she would cost per pound if she were a chicken, and fixed that sum as the masher's fine.

Under the Kansas Penal Code, anyone caught stealing chickens at night was charged with grand larceny. And anyone caught stealing chickens during the day was charged with petty larceny.

Check Out the Zebra

There's a zebra in Obbia, Somalia, that has unique stripes. This animal doesn't have the typical stripes associated with the species, rather vertical stripes that vary in width akin to those found on product bar codes.

It's a Dog's Life

In Tiajuana, Mexico, a police dog was discovered to be *on the take* for over eight years. The dog allowed dealers who secretly gave him filet mignon to pass suitcases of drugs over the border.

In South Bend, Indiana, Brutus was put on trial. Brutus was a guide dog who walked his masters into walls, pulled them down flights of stairs, and walked them into manholes. Brutus had three owners and he was finally brought to court and found guilty of manslaughter. Brutus was sentenced to death.

People who make ugly faces at dogs in Oklahoma will be fined and/or jailed.

In New Castle, Delaware, there's an anti-necking law that states: A couple may not neck—or even hold hands—while walking a dog on a leash.

In Fargo, North Dakota, six-year-old Collin Hazen invented a battery-powered dog collar that glows in the dark.

Screwed-Up Ostrich

Have you ever wondered why ostriches stick their heads underground? They think if they can't see their predators, their predators can't see them. In Lamu, Kenya, there's an ostrich that was so frightened, he corkscrewed his head and neck four feet into the ground for 21 days. A construction crew was hired to dig it out.

By the way, did you know that an ostrich can outrun a racehorse? When an ostrich is stretched out, it can cover 25 feet in one stride and can reach top speeds of almost 60 mph.

Peck Away, Woody

Monomoy Island, Massachusetts: On this small island, there's a woodpecker that hammers away all night, driving residents (literally) crazy. The divorce rate is far above average because people are always tired and cranky. Of the island's population of 320, sixteen are psychiatrists.

No More Monkey Business

Have you ever wondered why monkeys and rats clench their teeth? Well, the Office of Naval Research, the National Science Foundation, and the National Aeronautics and Space Administration found the answer. For $500,000 we now know that when monkeys and rats feel cheated, they get angry, scream and kick, and clench their jaws.

"Ribbit"

In Memphis, Tennessee, if a frog's croaking keeps you awake at night, you can have the frog arrested. In Hayden, Arizona, it's illegal to disturb a bullfrog. Go figure.

Deep Pockets

No, we're not talking about Donald Trump. We're talking about a female kangaroo in Tumbarumba, Australia, that has a pocket so deep, it can hold 245 cubic inches of cargo. "Karla" was purchased by a local zoo. She was trained to pick up litter and put it in her pouch.

11.
EAT, DRINK,
AND BE MERRY

SO, YOU'RE WITH THE LAW FIRM OF "EATT, DRINK & BeMERRY"? I'M WITH "CHEETUM & HOWELL".

Pearl-y Words

A man and woman were dining at a restaurant in Scranton, Pennsylvania. The woman ordered an oyster dish. The oyster contained a pearl that was valued at $750. Both the woman and the restaurant owner claimed they owned the pearl, and the case went to court. The judge, in his attempt to make an impartial ruling, awarded the pearl to the gentleman who paid for the woman's dinner.

A Nutty One

In Charlestown, South Carolina, it's illegal to eat nuts on a city bus. The maximum penalty for such an infraction can be 60 days in jail and a $500 fine.

Copyrats

Rats had a feast eating inside a $93,000 copy machine in the Cannon House Office Building. When the machine was opened up to find out why it wasn't working, an employee discovered that inside the copier were banana peels, corncobs, and a Hostess Twinkie still sealed in its plastic wrapping. With a $10,000 trade-in, a replacement machine cost the taxpayers an additional $97,000.

Amazing Alcohol

The National Institute on Alcohol Abuse and Alcoholism sponsored a project on aggressive behavior in fish after drinking alcohol. According to Dr. Harman Peeke, medical psychology professor at the University of California at San Francisco, fish were the only ethically acceptable subjects. It cost $102,000 to discover if sunfish that drink tequila are more aggressive then sunfish that drink gin.

Men in Nyala, Nevada, are forbidden to buy drinks for more than three people in any one round.

Since 1908, Mississippi has been known as a teatotaling state. However, the state collects taxes on liquor consumed in the state. This happens on the black market, where the law says that the state can collect a 10 percent tax on "any personal property the sale of which is prohibited."

Colossal Cuke

What's put Elbasan, Albania, on the map? It's the home of the world's largest cucumber—17 feet long. The cucumber has been bronzed and serves as a statue outside Elbasan City Hall.

All in the Ale

You can't serve beer (or any alcoholic beverage) to a moose in Alaska.

The *Encyclopedia Britannica* was banned in Texas because it disclosed the formula for making beer.

In North Dakota, it's against the law to serve beer with pretzels at any restaurant, bar, or club.

During the Oktoberfest Celebration in Germany, Jurgen Gerber took a six-day bath in warm beer. He didn't mind the smell because he worked in a brewery, but he did mind having wrinkled skin for three months. People claimed he looked like a ninety-year old.

Missouri legislators enacted a strict law that listed all the ingredients that can be used to brew beer. Don't worry about the beer being watered down—they forgot to include water as an ingredient.

How Sweet It Is

The National Aeronautics and Space Administration spent $200,000 to see if a sweet potato can be grown in outer space.

Ad This To the List

As part of its "Market Promotion Program," Uncle Sam picks up the tab for billions of advertising dollars. Our Uncle surely has his favorite nieces and nephews.

$5.1 million was given to Gallo Wines.
$1.1 million was given to Tyson Chickens.
$1 million was given to Ocean Spray.
$6.2 million was given to Blue Diamond Almonds. (Isn't that nuts?)
$465,000 was given to McDonald's.

Stinky Stuff

A woman in Jonesboro, Arkansas, was arrested for selling onions on Sunday; she was in violation of the local blue laws. The judge concluded that the woman was innocent because "an onion can sometimes take the place of a fruit, especially as dessert."

Say "Cheese"

In Wisconsin, apple pie cannot be served without a cheese topping.

HEY, ANYONE SEEN MY TIGHTS?

Speaking of Fruit...

Do you know how pink lemonade was invented? In 1857 Peter Conklin used a bucket of water in which a circus performer had soaked his red tights.

As Different as Apples and Oranges

How often have you heard combatants try to clarify their points of view by blurting out, "You're comparing apples to oranges." Well, the National Aeronautics and Space Administration (NASA) thought it was worth looking into this. NASA sponsored a team from Ames Research Center, Moffett Field, California, which compared Granny Smith Apples and Sunkist Navel Oranges. The team dried these fruits in a convection oven at a low temperature over the course of a few days. They then mixed these samples with potassium bromide and ground them in a mill. One hundred milligrams of the powders were thereafter pressed into a circular pellet. The findings? *Apples and oranges are very similar.* This should have a striking effect on future arguments and discussions.

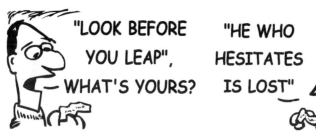

"LOOK BEFORE YOU LEAP", WHAT'S YOURS?

"HE WHO HESITATES IS LOST"

Fate and the Fortune Cookie

If you've eaten in a Chinese restaurant recently, you've probably received a fortune cookie along with the check. (By the way, fortune cookies are as American as apple pie.) The D & E Research Institute, Ithaca, New York, evaluated the effectiveness of the fortunes in these cookies.

The Institute contacted the owners of local Chinese restaurants, who agreed to help with this three-week study. This is how the deal went: After restaurant guests were given their checks, had divided up their cookies, and had read their fortunes, the waitperson would record their names, addresses, phone numbers, and the fortune that was written on the message tucked in the cookie. A year later these people were contacted and asked the following question:

In the last year, was the following statement [their fortune] true about your life?

Amazingly, 80% said that the fortune predicted came true.

Coffee Rouse

Porto Algre, Brazil: Coffee is so strong that just one cup will keep a person awake for 24 hours. If milk or cream is added, that will be reduced to 18 hours.

YOU'RE A HOT TOMATO, & I MEAN THAT IN THE BIBLICAL SENSE.

Biblical Babble

Rancho Cordova, California: The Vegetarianists Bible—yes, that's correct, a bible for Vegetarians—states in the first chapter that human beings evolved from the seeds of a single tomato plant.

Let 'Em Eat Cake

Prince Zabid, ruler of Qatar, boasts of having 612 wives. Of course, he can't remember their names, so he insists they wear numbers on their backs. The strange thing is that the prince is celibate. Why then would he want so many wives? He claims he marries so often because he likes eating wedding cake.

A Diet to Die for

In a jungle near the Cuchivero River in Venezuela, members of a small tribe have such large appetites that then often send their hunters 125 miles away to find someone to eat. (Yes, that's *someone,* not something.) They eat about six people a week. Every four years they elect a new leader and eat the old one.

In a Pickle

In Boston, Massachusetts, legislators said a pickle should bounce four inches when dropped from waist height.

In Los Angeles, California, they outlawed pickles altogether for fear the odor would offend people.

To be legal for sale in Connecticut, pickles must remain unbroken. They must bounce when dropped one foot above a solid oak table.

Knowing What
the Right Hand's Doing

Giuseppe Reggio claims to be the most proficient wine taster in the world. This resident of Naples, Italy, claims he can tell the country, region, vineyard, and row the grapes came from nine times out of ten. He can also tell if the grapes were picked with the right or left hand.

Ice Cream, You Scream...

In Newark, New Jersey, it's illegal to sell ice cream after 6 P.M. unless the customer has a doctor's note.

Methodist Church elders in Evanstown, Illinois, were pressured to forbid the sale of ice cream sodas because they believed that "soda water" was a "mite intoxicating."

Hilo, Hawaii: There's an ice cream shop that sells Chocolate Salmon Surprise. This ice cream is so awful that the shop serves the ice cream in buckets in case the customer "gives it back." The shop offers no refunds, but most people try this flavor out of curiosity.

And if you think that Chocolate Salmon Surprise isn't too appetizing, how about ice cream the Eskimos eat called "Cacpatok"? It's made of a mixture of edible greens, seal oil, reindeer fat, and snow.

What's Cooking
at the Pentagon?

After a six-month study, the Pentagon released its 22-page official brownie recipe. Here are some excerpts:

The texture of the brownie shall be firm but not hard.

Pour batter into a pan at a rate that will yield uncoated brownies which, when cut such as to meet the dimension requirements specified in regulation 3.4f, will weigh approximately 35 grams each.

The dimensions of the coated brownie shall not exceed 3½" x 2½" x $^5/_8$".

Shelled walnut pieces shall be of the small piece size classification, shall be of a light color, and shall be U.S. No. 1 of the U.S. Standards for Shelled English Walnuts. A minimum of 90 percent, by weight, of the pieces shall pass through a $^4/_{16}$-inch-diameter round hole screen and not more than 1 percent, by weight, shall pass through a $^2/_{16}$-inch-diameter round-hole screen.

And here's what the Pentagon had to say about the proper pumpkin filling: "Good consistency means that the canned pumpkin...after emptying from the container to a dry-flat surface...holds high mound formation, and at the end of ten minutes after emptying on such surface, the highest point of the mound is not less than 60 percent of the height of the container."

Flying Potato Chips

The Aerochip Institute, Mountain View, California, conducted experiments to test this age-old adage: *You can't throw a potato chip.* Given that the aerodynamic properties of potato chips may depend on their size, shape, weight, etc., a number of different chip types were tested. The long-awaited results are:

You can throw a potato chip, just not very far.

The distance traveled is largely dependent on chip weight, shape, and freshness.

Potato chips travel considerably farther when flying in formation, probably because such flight decreases the overall coefficient of drag.

All Bottled Up

Amos Sloane was shipwrecked on Rongerik Island in the South Pacific. He put a note in a bottle that complained of the intense heat and his steady diet of nothing but coconuts. The bottle floated more than 5,000 miles and was found by an Alaskan fisherman on Kodiak Island, in Alaska. Almost a year later Sloane found a bottle washed up on the beach. In it there was a note that read, "It's 20 below here, nothing to eat but frozen fish, and I have to work for a living, so don't complain."

(Under)Taking the Job Seriously

Harlan Pace is the proprietor of the Serenity Funeral Home in Tempe, Arizona. He makes sure that his "clients" are carefully groomed and their clothing matches the material that lines the coffin. Mr. Pace is so meticulous, he's a four-time recipient of the funeral business's prestigious Golden Casket Award.

Toothpick Toils

Kulang, China, runs seven centers for recycled toothpicks. People rummage through garbage cans to find toothpicks. They wash them, check for splinters, and are paid the equivalent of 35¢ a pound for reusable toothpicks.

SMOKEY, FOR THIS RECRUITMENT POSTER WE NEED YOU TO GET IN TOUCH WITH YOUR FEMININE SIDE.

Can't See the Forest for the Trees

The U.S. Forest Service was severely criticized for not hiring enough women as firefighters. The reasoning was that women weren't strong enough to lug the heavy firefighting equipment. When the EEOC got on its case, the Forest Service placed a job announcement stating that "Only unqualified applicants may apply." A second announcement stated that "Only applicants who do not meet [job requirement] standards will be considered."

PS: The *Washington Times* reported that many positions were not being filled because no qualified women were able to fill them.

Hailing the Hack

In Annapolis, Maryland, it's against the law for a cab driver to lock female passengers in their taxis. The law can impose a $500 fine and three years' probation.

Cab drivers must be careful whom they pick up in Magnolia, Arkansas. A local ordinance mandates that "Cab drivers may not knowingly carry a person of questionable or bad character to his or her destination."

Talking Teeth

Chicago Tribune columnist Mike Royko reported that charges were brought by the Americans with Disabilities Act against a private company because the company refused to hire a man who professed to have a microchip in one of his teeth. He claimed the microchip allowed him to communicate with people far, far away.

Tax Time

In 1994, just hours before the filing deadline, postal workers were collecting tax returns in a drive-through lane. A naked man drove up and handed his return to the postal worker. The postal worker quoted the man as saying, "Taxes this year have stripped me."

No More Pink Slips

In a 1994 speech, EEOC lawyer Davie Fram inferred that companies must exercise extreme caution when they discipline employees who attack their supervisors, because the employee may have a mental disability that the company must accommodate.

A Smash Hit

Naples, Italy: Giulio Lagomarsino has sung high notes reaching decibel levels of 105. He's shattered opera house light bulbs, eyeglasses of patrons in the audience, and he's even short circuited hearing aids.

Wheeling and Dealing

The Americans with Disabilities Act forced the owner of the Odd Ball Cabaret—a Los Angeles strip joint—to close because the dancing stall on the stage wasn't accessible to a stripper in a wheelchair.

This Seat's Taken

The EEOC deemed that obesity is protected under the Americans with Disabilities Act of 1990. Southwest Airline was sued by a 400-pound woman when an agent allegedly asked the woman to purchase two seats.

What foreSIGHT!

The Federal Highway Administration proposed a bill so that truck drivers who were blind in one eye and had poor vision in the other could get driver's licenses. (Fortunately a judge had the fore"sight" to see the perils of this bill and shot it down.)

Firefighting

In St. Louis, Missouri, it's illegal for an on-duty fireman to rescue a woman wearing a nightgown. If the woman wants to be rescued, she must be fully clothed.

Try Picking These Pockets

Monty Aylsworth is a clothing designer from Montclair, New Jersey. He designed a leather jacket that has 89 zippered pockets. There are pockets everywhere, including under the armpits. Mr. Aylsworth once wasted almost half an hour looking for money he had placed in one of his 89 pockets.

MS. FIPPS, I HAVE SOME DICTATION. WOULD YOU BRING IN YOUR STENO PAD AND YOUR MOTHER?

The Lap of Luxury

In Pasadena, California, a secretary can't be alone in a room with her boss.

Lost in the Translation

Ypsilanti, Michigan: A Japanese real estate company built 150 homes in Michigan hills. The head of the company, who spoke no English, needed to tell the building contractor that the dirt around the finished houses needed to be leveled. The translator, who spoke very little English, told the builder that "the houses needed to be leveled." The building contractor, who was paid by the hour, bulldozed all 150 houses.

Sticky Wicket

Baron, California: There's a cement floor in the Rialto Theater that hasn't been cleaned in seven years. It's so sticky from gum and candy that there's a crowbar placed under every seat so that theatergoers can unstick their shoes from the floor.

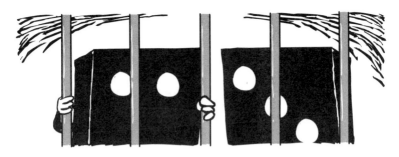

Never on Sunday

Dominos players should be careful about playing the game in Alabama on Sundays. It's illegal.

In Morristown, New Jersey, a merchant can sell custom-made drapery on Sunday, but can't sell the hardware to hang the drapery until Monday.

Taking the law to the extreme! In Nashville, Tennessee, police began enforcing the Sunday closing laws and many people were arrested. Judge Andrew Doyle claimed that on Sunday people could only do acts of charity. He ordered arrests for buses that were running, shows that were open, and preachers who were preaching. "We are going to close this town down," Judge Doyle exclaimed.

Restaurant owners beware. It's illegal to sell Limburger cheese on Sunday if you live in Houston, Texas, or to sell cherry pie à la mode if you live in Kansas.

Drugstores in Providence, Rhode Island, may sell toothbrushes on Sunday, but not toothpaste.

And in Columbus, Ohio, you can't legally sell corn flakes on Sunday.

13.
ON THE
POLITICAL TRAIL

Mark Twain once wrote: *"No man's life or property is safe while the Legislature is in session."* Perhaps the following will tell you why:

Let the Truth Prevail

Campaigners in Waterbury, Vermont, are prohibited from "telling lies or fabricating stories" while on the campaign trail. (*I'm having difficulty refraining from an editorial comment.*)

State of Confusion

When the state of Oklahoma was first organized, legislators spent 88 out of the first 90 days arguing over the location of the capital. During the two remaining days, frivolous laws were passed. One empowered the territory to license sea pilots. Another prohibited anyone from fishing for whales off the coast.

Political Potpourri

In Maryland, two legislators, ironically named Masters and Johnson, recently introduced a bill to create a board to license sex therapists.

Voters in McCook, Nebraska, aren't allowed to show up at the polls on roller skates. And in Texas no one's allowed to carry a spear or sword to the polls.

Politicians in both Oxford and Cleveland, Ohio, passed rules making it a violation for women to wear patent leather shoes.

Food for Thought

Missouri legislators actually spent time selecting an official watermelon inspector. The person's official title would be "The Official Plugger, Muncher, and Taster of the State of Missouri."

In Sugartown, Louisiana, politicians must refrain from squirting tobacco juice on the sidewalk while on the campaign trail.

Politicians in Preston, Idaho, aren't allowed to eat onions before speaking before a large group of voters within the city limits.

In Crookston, Minnesota, voters are banned from nibbling on popcorn while listening to a political speech.

A Utah legislator proposed a resolution that every television meteorologist buy an ice cream cone for every member of the House of Representatives whenever the forecast was wrong. (The resolution, however, failed.)

No one in Sidney, Ohio, is allowed to carry a "a sack of Spanish peanuts" to a political rally or chew the peanuts while the candidate is speaking.

Dress for Success

All politicians in Fairfield, Illinois, must wear shirts with buttons running up the front when they're running for public office.

In San Angelo, Texas, all campaigners must wear long pants when walking down the streets or shaking hands with prospective voters.

Any woman in Wheatfield, Indiana, who's seen wearing shorts, a halter, or bathing suit to a political rally can be found guilty of a misdemeanor.

And any adult who strolls around barefoot at a political rally in Elizabethtown, Kentucky, had better BEWARE!

All in the Game

A local ordinance in Atwoodville, Connecticut, prohibits people from playing Scrabble while waiting for a politician to start speaking.

Candidates in Clewiston, Florida, aren't allowed to play chess to pass the time.

14.
JUST BY COINCIDENCE...

"**coincidence** *n.*
an accidental occurrence
of related or identical
events, ideas, etc."

Home Is Where the Heart Is

Mr. and Mrs. L. Willsey, of Sacramento, California, had been hunting for their dream house. As they checked the classifieds, they found such a house. They called the broker only to learn that it was an ad for their house that they'd put on the market a month earlier. The search for their dream house ended!

Case for Crash Helmets

Aeschylus was famous for writing more than 70 Greek tragedies. He was once told by a prophet that he would die from a blow from heaven. So, Aeschylus never went outdoors during a storm. He was killed outside in Gela, Sicily, on a beautiful, sunny day when an eagle, mistaking his bald head for a rock, dropped a huge tortoise on him to break its shell.

Five-Time Winners

Ralph and Carolyn Cummins, of Clintwood, Virginia, had five children, single births. All were born on February 20.

These Are No Fish Tales

In 1903, Madame Eduigue Rereit, of Paris, France, was washing dishes when her favorite ring slid down the drain. It was washed into the river and swallowed by a fish. How was that discovered? Madame Rereit purchased the fish and found the ring when she was cleaning it for dinner.

Mel Cohen, of Gravois Mills, Missouri, was cleaning a bass he caught. In the fish, he found the *mezuzah* (a Jewish religious symbol posted on door frames) that he had lost five months earlier.

Ralph Rigdon, of Mystic, Connecticut, lost his worker's ID badge while fishing 30 feet off Long Island Sound. Two months later, fishing in the same spot, he hooked the badge.

C. Dornqwast, of Wolf River, Wisconsin, lost a key chain with several keys. He found it a year later when he caught a six-pound pike.

Oh, No, Not Another Fish Story...

Maggie Jacobs lost her great-grandmother's ring while working in a vegetable garden. She found the ring six years later when she picked two radishes that had grown together with the ring encircling them.

Briefcase of Mistaken Identity

Paul DeVries, of Daly City, California, was playing golf one day when he found a briefcase containing $5,000 worth of bonds registered to Paul DeVries of San Francisco. The two men aren't related and had never met. (Do you think they ever bonded?)

Jumping Jupiter

Three fragments of the Shoemaker-Levy 9 comet impacted Jupiter 25 years after three crucial events in the Apollo-11 moon landing mission.

The first fragment impacted exactly 25 years to the day of the Apollo-11 launch.

The largest fragment hit Jupiter 25 years to the minute of the Apollo-11 landing.

The final fragment hit almost precisely 25 years after the Apollo-11 lift-off from the lunar surface.

Perfect Attendance

Stuart Carter was a senior about to graduate from Roseburg High School, in Oregon. He was scheduled to win an award for perfect attendance throughout his school years, but was absent on the day the award was given out.

15.
HONEST ABE

Ask someone to name the tenth president of the United States or perhaps the eighteenth, and you'll probably get a blank stare. Yet ask someone to name the sixteenth president, and "Abraham Lincoln" pops out. There are many coincidences associated with this famous president. Here are a few you might find of interest:

Presidential Jobs

The jobs Abe Lincoln had before he took office spell
"president."

rail s **p** litter

rive **r** man

deputy surv **e** yor

po **s** tmaster

leg **i** slator

sol **d** ier

groc **e** r

attor **n** ey

representa **t** ive

Lucky 7 (?)

The number 7 is attributed to Abraham Lincoln over
and over again. Could that be coincidental?

His ancestors came from Hingham, England. (There
are seven letters in each name.) He lived in Kentucky
for seven years, and in Salem for seven years. He was
sworn into Congress on December 7, 1847, and held
seven offices. He spent seven years in state legislature,
appointed seven cabinet ministers, and seven states
seceded. He had seven debates with Stephen Douglas
(who has seven letters in each name). And he died a
few minutes after seven on the seventh day of the
month.

Coincidentally, each of his names, Abraham Lincoln,
has seven letters.

ABE and JFK

The following similarities have been linked to the lives and deaths of Abraham Lincoln and John F. Kennedy. Many of them happened 100 years apart.

Lincoln was elected to Congress in 1846. Kennedy was elected to Congress in 1946.

Lincoln was elected president in 1860. Kennedy was elected president in 1960.

The names Lincoln and Kennedy each contain seven letters.

Both were particularly concerned with civil rights.

Both had children die while they were living in the White House.

Both were shot on a Friday.

Both were shot in the head.

Both were shot in the presence of their wives.

The secretaries of both presidents warned them not to go to the theater and Dallas, respectively.

Lincoln's secretary was named Kennedy. Kennedy's secretary was named Lincoln.

Both were assassinated by Southerners.

Both were succeeded by Southerners named Johnson.

Andrew Johnson, who succeeded Lincoln, was born in 1808. Lyndon Johnson, who succeeded Kennedy, was born in 1908.

John Wilkes Booth, who assassinated Lincoln, was born in 1839. Lee Harvey Oswald, who assassinated Kennedy, was born in 1939. Both assassins were known by their three names totaling 15 letters.

Booth ran from the theater and was captured in a warehouse. Oswald ran from the warehouse and was captured in a theater.

Booth and Oswald were assassinated before their cases came to trial.

Lincoln was killed in Ford's Theater. Kennedy was killed in a Lincoln Convertible made by the Ford Motor Co.

President of the Week

Important events happened on specific days of the week. Abraham Lincoln:

> was born on *Sunday*
> was first elected to office on *Monday*
> was first elected president on *Tuesday*
> was admitted to the bar on *Wednesday*
> delivered the Gettysburg Address on *Thursday*
> was shot on *Friday*
> died on *Saturday*

16.
ETC., ETC., ETC.

Splish, Splash

There's a law in Lander, Wyoming, that prohibits people from taking a bath when the cold weather sets in. However, adults are allowed to bathe once a month, children not at all.

Morristown, Vermont, prohibits people from taking baths unless they've gotten permission from the Board of Selectmen.

In the state of Wisconsin, there's a law stating that "Every proprietor of a lumber camp must supply an individual bathtub for each lumberjack in his employ."

A woman in Crawfordsville, Indiana, sued for divorce. She claimed her husband had a habit of bringing his friends into their bathroom while she was in the tub.

In Virginia it's illegal to take a bath in a tub if the tub is located in any room attached to the house.

All bathtubs installed in the state of Maine must have four legs. If it doesn't have any legs, it must be installed outside the home.

Mastery

The *Chicago Tribune* reported that in various parts of the country it's verboten for realtors to use the term "master bedroom" because it connotes slavery.

Military Mania

Maine Senator William Cohen and Delaware Senator William Roth announced that the Navy was paying $640 for a toilet seat that would cost us only $25. And then there's the $400 hammer and $54 stapler.

The National Aeronautics and Space Administration (NASA) spent $23 million to build a prototype toilet for the space shuttle. The price tag represented a 900 percent increase over the original estimate because the astronauts wanted a manual flush rather than an automatic one.

Not Rain, Nor Snow...

In May of 1942, Emanuel Ehrlich of Jacksonville, Florida, mailed a letter at the post office. It was returned to him marked "undeliverable" by the U.S. Postal Service 29 years later.

General Zachary Taylor nearly lost the presidential nomination. The letter asking him to accept the office was returned unopened by General Taylor because it was stamped "postage collect."

About the Author

During my professional career, I've been an English and paralegal teacher, technical writer, marketing communications specialist, and training guru. But the most important and rewarding job I've had is being mom to my two wonderful sons, Marc and Eric Lindsell. Marc lives in San Francisco, California, and is an incredible architect. Eric is a dedicated and caring chiropractor who lives and practices in Columbia, Maryland.

I've written about a dozen books for the professional market. My entree into the humor market was with my hot seller *Loony Laws & Silly Statutes,* published by Sterling. This book continues to receive national acclaim on talk shows and in such publications as *Woman's Day, Sun, National Enquirer,* and *Entrepreneur.*

My husband Jon and I make our home west of Boston in *Parnassus*—the beautiful home our son Marc designed. When I'm not writing, I enjoy sailing, traveling, painting, sailing, photographing nature, sailing, eating strawberry cheesecake, and skiing. And yes, sailing!

Sheryl Lindsell-Roberts, M.A.

INDEX